Survival *of the* Lamb Against *all* Odds

A Personal Memoir

Savio Allan Lamb

INDIA · SINGAPORE · MALAYSIA

ISBN 979-8-89067-940-6

CONTENTS

PROLOGUE

Survival of the Lamb against all odds is a heartfelt autobiography that takes readers through the trials and triumphs of the writer's life. It is a testament to the power of resilience, faith, and the enduring spirit to overcome obstacles and transform them into stepping stones of success. The author's experiences serve as a source of inspiration and motivation for readers to navigate their own challenges with strength, grace, and unwavering determination.

Chapter 1

MY CHILDHOOD DAYS

Life Begins with You Leaving Your Mother's Womb Crying.

No one can truly fathom the journey that life has in store for us. This book is a chronicle of my life's journey with its many ups and downs, good times, and bad times—a common man's extraordinary journey through life. Where I held onto a never-die attitude, facing even the biggest obstacles with unwavering belief. I always saw a silver lining, counting my blessings one by one, and appreciating what God has bestowed upon me, even amidst life's struggles.

I hope that by reading my story readers will be inspired to face their own struggles and never give up on the beautiful life God has blessed them with. It's essential to value and make the most of our journey through life, especially when millions around the world are going through their worst times. Especially during the pandemic and the War in Ukraine and in other parts of the world where millions of human beings including kids are going through hell.

As a baby, I was always filled with happiness, joy, and peace, and my parents loved me to the moon. I was the youngest of four siblings, two elder sisters, and a brother. Being the youngest, I was pampered and cherished by all.

The lovely memories of my childhood include my dad making me cargo ship of metal models, as he was a welder in a shipping yard in Mazgon Docks, Mumbai, where ships were built and repaired. I also remember him carrying me on his back like a horse, galloping throughout our small abode. His smoking tricks, blowing perfect smoke circles, always amazed me. He was a very good musician too, whose voice was similar to Bollywood singer of the 60 and 70 s the late Mukesh ji. He used to sing on stage playing the harmonica. He was also a great carpenter and electrician. Every furniture in my house was built by his own hands. He was skilled in so many talents and a very cool person with a big heart. He used to play the harmonium along with other instruments. He loved me dearly and was very fond of me. I have this strong feeling that my elder son Aarav is his reincarnation who God has sent back to me.

This belief came to my mind when as a kid I took him for the first time to my dad's place for a visit. He was sleeping in the car during the drive but woke up as soon as we reached my dad's place. My dad place is on the third floor which has no lifts, so we took him walking up. When he reached the first floor, he turned to me and told me that he has been here before, when it was the first time, we took him to the building ever. This made me believe that my dad, is indeed sent by God to me as my son. I feel God works wonders and makes all things beautiful in his own time. Similarly, my second son Vivaan I believe is a reincarnation of my father in law's younger brother who had died in a road accident. A truck ran over him, when he was a little boy holding my father in laws hands walking on the road . My son has the same features of my Father in law, even his ways of doing things like sleeping or walking or standing pose, which are similar to my father in Law . I may be wrong but that what's it feels like to me. Maybe those loved ones in our lives who are taken from us abruptly are sent back to us through another person to spend some more precious times with us. I am sure many in the world would be having the same experiences.

My parents and siblings loved me dearly, and I reciprocated that love with all my heart.

My mom's delicious Goan food and my grandmother's Anglo Indian ball curry with rice and pepper fry were simply unforgettable. The mere thought of those dishes makes my mouth water even today.

Family and friends would visit our home on many occasions, especially during Christmas. We, the kids, would stay up all night making Christmas delicacies, sharing joyful moments. My parents used to go for Christmas dances at Byculla Mechanics, the most happening place during those times for dances. I remember my aunt and her fiance Joseph uncle, a thorough gentleman and remarkable ballroom dancer who won many dance contests with my stylish aunty Violet, in her miniskirts and long leather boots, who resembled the popular Bollywood star of that time, Zeenat Aman.

Visiting my dad's place near the Victorian styled structure of Gloria Church in a place called Byculla in Bombay, was always delightful. We witnessed the burning of an effigy at midnight on New Year's, symbolizing the end of the old and the beginning of the new.

We used to live in a building called Taj Mansion on Sankli Street. There used to be an Iranian Restaurant there on the ground floor which served the best chai and Bun Maska Pau, which I relished and is etched in my childhood memories.

This place was so vibrant and lively with lots of catholic living there. Christmas times used to be so festive with lots of decorations on the lanes with big stars lit up everywhere on every lane. There used to stars with lights on individual houses too. We had a great time living here.

My Dad lived with his mom, sisters, and grandmother. While my father was growing up here a tragedy happened in his family. His younger brother who was a baby had fallen from the balcony and died tragically. My Dad never recovered from that trauma and decided to shift our new residence to the suburbs of Mumbai.

My Dad purchased a place in a place called Nehru Nagar in Kurla East. We four kids spent our childhood there. It was a beautiful place with Jamun trees planted front of our home. We remember climbing this tree and plucking the juicy jamuns. We used to enjoy all the festivals there be it Diwali, Ganapati, or Eid celebrations as we had neighbours of all religions living together as one big family in peace. I loved the Ganapati festivals as the area being more of Maharashtrian population every society complex, around us used to keep Big Ganapati statues and the place used to get so festive during Ganapati festivals. I used to love the Modak which used to be served by our neighbours to us. They were hot steamy momos like pieces, with sweet juicy coconut masala inside. It used to melt in my mouth. We were so fond of it that my sister's learnt the art of making it in a pressure cooker and we relished it so much.

The other festival celebrated was Janmashtami, where dahi handi, small pot with curd used to be tied on every society or apartment blocks as high as possible. The whole day different, team of youngster used to try to break the handi and get their hands on the cash prize hung with the dahi handi. It was so famous that the Spanish teams also started visiting our city in Mumbai to take up the challenge. This festival signified Lord Krishnas playfulness of getting curd in his childhood from the handi (vessel) in which the curd used to be stored at a height. He used to break the handi to eat the curd inside it. The same tradition was followed till today during the Janmashtami festivals.

Then we had the Holi festivals where the everyone used to burn pile wood stacked in a tent shape. The next day there used to be Holi cebration where everyone used to celebrate with colours of different kinds either by applying it on each other or by filling water ballons and throwing at each other. It was such a colourful celebration that we as kids used to have so much fun playing with all our family and friends.

A funny incident I would like to share during Holi Puja, when piles of wood was burned and Puja was preformed, few folks threw coins in it. The next morning I decided to collect the coins from the hole that was dug to burn the wood. I put my feet on the wood thinking it was cold But the embers was still hot and burning . My whole sole got burned as the wood was still hot. I just jumped out of it and ran home and applied Burnol all over my sole which had swelled up in boils. I once again paid the price of being naughty and could not retrieve any of the coins thrown inside the fire the night before during Puja.

The Eid festivals also used to be awesome where during Bakri Eid, we celebrated with our neighbors who shared awesome Goat meat with us the next day. We used to relish the Mutton Biryani they used to prepare and send to our home.

Even the sweet dish called Sheer Kurma or Sewai which used to be shared by our neighbours during Eid. It used to be my favourite sweet dish. My mother too used to make it for me every time she visited me during Christmas. I still remember the taste of it and think of her whenever I eat it even today.

The best festival I loved was Christmas, just because I knew my mother would be visiting me to share Birthday of Jesus. I used to look forward to it. The Christmas tree decorations, wearing new clothes and mostly getting gifts from Santa. It was a dream come true just to have my mom by my side. There were few times when she could not visit us due to her job demand. Those were the saddest days of my life. But she used to make it up by coming next month for my birthday which fell on 27 January. She made sure she organized a nice party for me with music, cake and a lovely gift.

Another delicacy that our whole family relished was the faloodas. we had an awesome shop in Kurla West, which used to make the most awesome faloodas with so much different choices that we used to just find ways to go and eat faloodas in that place, which sadly is no more there. The falooda I tasted there I have never tasted anywhere in my life till date. My search is still on for the same flavour that I tasted in my old favourite restaurant.

We as kids had a great time during the rainy season in Mumbai. Especially as the first thing that closed during the heavy rains was our school. I was in a Co Ed school called Kedarnath Vidhya Prasarni (KVP) High school which was just walking distance from my place. I studied here till sixth grade. Our classrooms used to be on the ground floor which used to get flooded as soon as there was a heavy downpour. We used to run and play in the rain. There used to be so much rain that small pools used to be formed in the opposite society ground. We kids used to go and swim there during the rains. It used to be so much fun. It was my first experience of swimming in a pool formed due to the heavy rains. We kids used to make paper boats and leave it on the stream of water flowing by street side.

One day it rained so heavily accompanied with thunder and lightning that we kids got scared thinking our building would collapse. We all four started saying our rosary together and as we finished our rosary the rains had eased off, which gave us some relief. These incidents made my faith stronger and reminded me about what my mother used to say, that God always heard the prayers of little children.

I still remember the Desouza family staying a floor below us. One of the kids from that family was my class mate. Their dad without fails every evening at 7 pm used to say the rosary with his 3 kids and wife. I could hear it whenever I passed their house. Today all the three kids are settled in USA as engineers and doing well in life. Which made me realize the importance of family praying together. It is said, the family which prayers together stays together That's one of the reasons I make it a point to pray every evening with my family. My life in that place in Kurla was a truly great experience for the rest of my life.

Life was truly awesome until my dad decided to move to Bahrain for a job change, drawn by the then allure of the Gulf's promising opportunities. Little did we know that this move would lead to a heart-wrenching blow when he tragically passed away in a hit-and-run car accident in Bahrain. I couldn't even attend his funeral service, as my mom was in a state of shock. I was in Mumbai, as a four-year-old kid along with my siblings, with my grandparents who did not know how to give us this tragic news.

Our lives took a sharp turn for the worst. Friends and even some family acquaintances vanished, avoiding the responsibility of supporting my mom in raising us four kids alone in this cold and heartless world. One of these deserters even advised my mom to give us up for adoption. However, my mother bravely rejected the idea and made up her mind to bring us up by herself, with the unwavering protection and guidance of Mother Mary and Jesus.

Our childhood days, without having our parents near us, felt sometimes like hell Especially when my mom's cheque used to get delayed, while on transit from the gulf. We at times didn't have food at home, sometimes for the whole day, and our neighbours seeing us kids hungry used to send some food across. God bless them for that always.

We had some real good neighbours living with us. But there was also one of them who was a vulture preying on us kids knowing, we just had grandparents taking care of us. He is dead now and surely. rotting in hell, as he was the one who sexually molested me as a kid. I hope and pray that he did not do the same to my sister's or brother or to the other kids in our society. It happened just on one or two occasions but it's enough to scare you for the rest of your life. I have mentioned it in my book as I am sure it happens to many kids even today but who never mention it to their parents or guardians for reasons beyond their control and understanding. I am glad that Laws have been enacted to bring this menace in control and punish the perpetrators of sexual abuse on kids like, The POCSO Act, which stands for Prevention of Children from Sexual Offences Act enacted in 2012, which is a blessing for kids nowadays . I hope and pray kids especially the young ones are educated about good touch and bad touch so that they can expose such sexual offenders immediately without they feeling guilty or ashamed in any way. This is one of the injustices I plan to fight against once I start my own Law Practice in Mumbai.

It was also one of the reasons I never let my kids out of my sight for too long. I have educated them how to deal with such situations if ever they come across it. They being boys makes no difference as these sexual predators treat both the boys and girls the same way. I am glad that they have been spared of such sick acts, especially because God has protected them always and having their parents around also plays a very important role which was not the case for me during my childhood days.

These were few of the bad experiences I had as a kid. But these bad phase of my life, made me a better human being and stronger mentally to face the cold world as we grew up. My mom kept taking each of my siblings one by one to the gulf after they finished their studies. They are still there today doing well for themselves. My brother who went to the gulf initially has migrated to Canada and doing well for himself having a beautiful life there with his loving family in Vancouver.

Today, we four of us are well-settled and thriving in our respective lives, spread all over the world. As for me, I have been living my dream job, presently as an Assistant Commissioner of Customs and GST, in the Central Government of India. I have been enjoying the beautiful city of Bengaluru which my wife and kids love so much that, they have decided to settle here for life. As for me born a Bombay boy I still yearn to be in Mumbai, but will eventually end up in Bengaluru as for me family always came first, before anything else my life.

Chapter 2

MY MOM, MY ROCK

Dedicated to my mom.

In this chapter, I recount the immense pain my mom endured when she lost her husband, leaving behind four young children. I was just 4 years old and my sibling too were small. Those days there were no insurance claims which my mom could use to help her tide away the difficult times ahead. Despite the heartbreak and the tragic fate, she never gave up and became a fighter, raising us on her own with her unwavering faith in God and especially in Mary Help of Christians and the power of saying the rosary which has always helped me throughout my life. My mother worked at the Taj Mahal Hotel in Mumbai, and later moved to the UAE to provide a better life for us.

I recall fond memories of spending time with her, writing letters to her when she was abroad, and cherishing the moments together during Christmas vacations. Her love and sacrifices for us were boundless, even when it meant fulfilling my shopping list, leading to my indulgence in chocolates and subsequent visits to the dentist.

We had a memorable childhood in our Dad's place in Mumbai, playing various games and studying together during exams. My passion for cricket eventually paved the way for my love for hockey later in life.

Despite some mischievous incidents at school, where once I was caught by 5th grade class teacher for stealing tiffin, from few girls of my class. She called my mom who was so upset, as she used to give me nice meals in my tiffin box. She slapped me in front of the whole class, for the first and only time in my entire life. She felt hurt that in spite of her giving me tiffin, I being greedy use to eat from the other girl's tiffins too. I never did it again, as saw my mother in tears after she slapped me. She hugged me and took me in her arms on my way back home from school. My mom's love and support shaped me into who I am today. She was the pillar of my strength and eventual success in life. I believe she is in heaven, watching over me and showering her blessings on me and my family. Her passing in 2012 was a difficult time for me. She had her second heart attack in UAE and her ambulance arrived late and was even stuck in traffic due to which she passed away in the ambulance itself before she could reach the hospital. Earlier when she had suffered her first heart attack a few years back, she was in Mumbai where my neighbours were quick to take her to the hospital which saved her life. Maybe if she was staying with me in Mumbai, I could have saved her life, and she would have lived longer, spending it with me. But destiny had something else stored for her. Maybe my dad wanted her in heaven sooner than later. He loved my mom very much and had four beautiful kids with her. She married my dad when she was just sixteen and were a loving couple till my dad met the tragic accident. It must have been so heart wrenching and difficult for her to lose the love of her life at such a tender age. But she kept on fighting for all of us with the world. She gave her everything to bring us all up in a nice way. Her strength and determination continue to inspire me. Sadly, I could not attend even her funeral which was held in UAE, due to circumstances beyond my control.

I am grateful to God for giving me such a brave and loving mother who worked tirelessly to ensure all her children were well-settled in life. My brother Allwin excels in his career as a Chef in Vancouver, Canada with a loving wife Lorie and beautiful kids Jaiden and Ella. The rest of our family is settled in the UAE. As for me, I have been living my dream job as an Assistant Commissioner of Customs under the sports quota, allowing me ample time with my family and to play my favourite sports hockey and later badminton. I picked up this beautiful game without any coaching by just watching badminton coaching on YouTube and matches of players. I have being playing in Nationals of Masters Badminton last 10 years and will be playing till 70 plus if my body can hold on to the injuries, I have suffered down the road. For me just playing at that age will be a proud feeling. So, whether I win any laurels or not is not important so far as I am enjoying and loving the game. I just believe in giving it your best and leaving the rest on God. The best part of it is making good friends along the way and cherishing those memories by taking photos of myself and the other players in the circuit.

The selfies taken by me of players, always brings a smile on their faces during the stress of playing the tournaments.

I owe everything I am to my mom, my rock, and thank her and God for the love and support that shaped my life. I dedicated this song to my mom which I used to sing to her as a kid. It's used to bring tears to her eyes, but every word of this beautiful song fit my mom perfectly. It goes like this.

Mother of mine you gave to me,

all of my life to do as I please,

I owe everything I have to you,

Mother sweet mother of mine.

Mother of mine when I was young

You showed me the right way
things had to be done.
Without your arms where would I be,
Mother sweet mother of mine.
Mother of mine now I am grown,
and I can walk straight all on my own.
I'd like to give you,
what you gave to me.
Mother sweet mother of mine.
Mother you gave me happiness,
much more than words can say,
I pray to the lord that he may bless you
every night and every day.

CHAPTER 3

FOND MEMORIES OF BOARDING LIFE

My Boarding life at St. Don Bosco, Matunga, in Bombay was truly the best days of my life. I was a mischievous and naughty child, which led my grandparents to decide that my brother and I should be enrolled in the boarding school.I would like to mention that my brother was an angel compared to me as a kid. I was the mischievous kind and my brother had to pay the price for it. Like when as kids I use to steal money which my mom used to send, from our home cupboard and my sister being older used to punish me and my brother thinking one of us did it. They used to make us kneel on salt rocks, for more than an hour. But even then I never admitted taking the money to have falooda at my favourite restaurant.

On another occasion I crushed my sister's glass bangles, she had worn on her hands fighting for sweets, and my brother tried to come to her rescue and I pushed him back on bed where he was playing his guitar. He fell on his guitar and it broke. I still have that sad image of him seeing his guitar broken in my mind and before he went into a rage to whack me. I ran out of the house. Later when things were peaceful, I got fevicol to get his guitar repaired and made peace with him.

I remember so vividly playing cricket with my brother with wet socks tied together to form a ball in our balcony. He was a great bowler and remember him giving our Don Boscos school cricket wicket keeper a black eye with his fast bowling while keeping wickets.

Once I sadly remember my grandfather beating him with his leather belt, as someone in our building falsely accused him of stealing the locks of the terrace door, inspite of him pleading his innocence in tears.

Similarly, I was once trashed with a cane by my aunty for breaking a Red Label bottle when she arrived from Bahrain. As I opened the cartoon from the wrong end and the bottle slipped and broke in to pieces, spilling the alcohol all over the floor. The cane marks were itched on my hands after the beating.

These were the few mischievous incidents that made us end up in a boarding school which later turned out to be a blessing in disguise to both me and my brother.

During a visit to the school for admissions, with my siblings and cousin brother Walter, we encountered the Rector, Fr. Dennis Duarte. He turned out to be a saintly man with a divine smile. Impressed by our good marksheets, he granted us admission instantly. It felt like a miracle, and my mother's prayers had worked once again. This changed the course of our lives forever.

The initial days in the boarding were a bit tough. We had dormitories with individual beds and common washrooms for more than 50 kids. The study hall overlooked a beautiful green hockey field, which became a blessing for us, as we were passionate about sports. The best part of it was that the Mumbai Customs Hockey team used to practice on it. It made me realize, what level of hockey I would have to play to get into their team, so that I could get a Customs officers job through sports quota.

The best part of boarding was the dining room, where we had three full meals, and tea-time snacks felt like heaven. I particularly enjoyed the Italian biscuits, jam, butter, and porridge. On festive occasions, the food was even more special, especially the mouth-watering biryanis and delicious South Indian dishes like masala dosas and idlis. However, I developed a dislike for pork due to a drunken cook who failed to clean the pork hair out properly.

I often envied the dining room of the priests on the floor above ours and even considered becoming a priest at one point, but the then Rector advised me against doing so solely for the sake of dining privileges.

Feast days were fantastic, as they began with music, and we enjoyed fun-filled games all day long. I cherished these moments my entire life. However, the only downside of boarding life was missing my mom, who was working in the Gulf to provide us with the best possible upbringing.

Boarding life introduced me to soccer and hockey, which became my passions. On my first day of soccer with the boarders, I fell and tore my favorite blue trousers. But I got up and continued to play, determined to improve. I remember Fr Anneclet, who was the Administrator of the school. He used to give us free hockey sticks and football boots which had studs of wood which had to be fixed by nails. It's not the fancy ones of Nike, Addidas and Puma brand my kids wear while playing their football in school. In our case the nails used to go through our soles and hurt us when the football shoes used to.get worn out playing in the rains and muck.

My brother and I started in the under-13 soccer B team, but we quickly improved in both football and hockey and became stars for our respective teams, winning several tournaments. Our coaches, including our Rector Fr. Chrisogolus and Father Annaclet who, motivated and supported us wholeheartedly by giving us free kits, jerseys, stocking etc. Without which I would never be able to play hockey or football. I also followed the teachings of our religion teacher and stayed focused on my sports and studies.

My brother excelled in soccer and became the best goalkeeper of Don Bosco and the Mumbai under-17 team. However, due to the politics in Indian sports and the uncaring attitude of officials towards players, he gave up his soccer career.

In contrast, I thrived in hockey and became a skilled defender. I could dribble past the entire opposition team and score a goal for my school team. Eventually, I captained the under-16 team and led them to victory in the Fr. Donnelly Cup, scoring the winning goal in the semi-final. I would like to mention about Sir Jaswant Singh, who coached me in hockey at Khalsa college grounds, during our summer holidays. It was a blessing to hockey players, few of whom represented India like Joaquim Carvalho, Marcelus Gomes, and many more like Happy Ful, Angela Dsa who represented the Indian women's hockey team.

Our school's rigorous training and hard work paid off, and we won several championships in soccer and hockey. As a treat, the Coaches and Father's would take us to a famous South Indian restaurant called Madras Cafe, where they allowed us to order whatever was on the menu unlimited to our hearts content.

In one particularly successful year, we won the treble, Interschool championships in soccer, lifting the under-13, under-15, and under-17 trophies in the year 1984. Our team pictures were featured in The Sports Star Illustrated magazine, a proud moment we cherish to this day.

The boarding school also organized an overnight picnic to Gorai beach, known as the Goa of Mumbai, where we enjoyed a delicious prawn biryani treat from nearby nuns, who were close to Salesians of Don Bosco.

One of the few naughty things I did in the boarding was that one day I kept an onion under my arm pit and slept thinking I was going to get fever in the morning as advised by another naughty boarder. In the morning Father came on his rounds to wake up all the boarders and asked me why I was not getting dressed for school. I told him I have fever. He touched my fore head to check my temperature. My body temp was normal. I checked to see where the onion had gone, it was lying under the bed. I had no choice but to go to school as my attempt to bunk school didn't work. I never ever tried to bunk school ever again.

Another naughty episode which back fired on me was when I was imitating Brother Loyola our class teacher in the boarding, who unfortunately was standing behind me. No one warned me from the class, as I was busy imitating him. When I turned around, he slapped me so hard that I could see stars in the daylight. Fortunately, It was the only slap I got when in the boarding school.

Another naughty episode was when I was standing with another boarder in a queue for food in the refectory. He jokingly hit my head with a spoon on my head. I retaliated by playfully hitting him on the head with a fork instead of a spoon. Blood started spurting like a fountain from the back of his head. I ran away after that, to school to avoid the wrath of the Administrator of the Boarding school, Brother Rocha, who had a very bad temper and would have cobbled me if I had met him instantly. Therefore wisely, I left for school and luckily by evening it must not crossed his mind to summon me again. I was saved once again from a thrashing from Brother Rocha. Who was a very kind soul, who played football along with us and I remember him getting VCR for us to watch movies in the Boarding from his trip to Italy.

Despite all these playful incidents, I had a lot of fun at St Don Bosco. The boarding life instilled discipline, teamwork, and independence, making us better equipped to face life's challenges.

I have countless fond memories of my boarding days, and each one is cherished for the rest of my life. Boarding life at St. Don Bosco, Matunga, shaped me into the person I am today, and I am forever grateful for the opportunities it provided. It was through Don Bosco that I gained admission to St. Xavier's College, one of the best colleges in Mumbai and the second-best phase of my life.

I never ever touched alcohol either in school or my entire life. I had promised my mom that I would never drink alcohol or smoke and one day become a Customs Officer. So that she does not get hassled at the airport by Customs, while visiting me during her annual visits.

The promise to join Customs was made by me to my mother, when, during one of her earlier visits while she waited 2 hours at the red channel. Those days in the early 70s there was no green channel facilities for international passengers specially the ones coming from gulf countries. I could watch her ordeal from the viewing gallery above the customs baggage hall whenever I went to receive her at Sahar International airport, Mumbai.

I kept all my promises I made to my mom, thank God for that. Hope she is proud of me in heaven.

The boarding school was like heaven for me and my brother who grew taller and stronger as the years went by. Every weekend our family used to come to visit us. I used to miss my mom always, and continued writing letters to her regularly. I was in the boarding school, from seventh grade to tenth grade. I enjoyed every second of those four years. During which time I grew much closer to Mother Mary to whom I always went to pray in the Shrine of St Don Boscos dedicated to Mother Mary (The most peaceful place in the world to pray till date for me). Before every exam, matches or any important events in my life, like before the selection trials for the Mumbai hockey team for the Junior Nationals. My prayers were always answered and I got to play for the Mumbai hockey team two years in a row, which eventually made me realize my dream of playing for the Mumbai Customs hockey team, and becoming a Customs officer under sports quota on 26.2.91. On that day I wore my white uniform for the first day. It was a moment of great pride for my mom, who framed my passport seize picture wearing the white customs officers uniform. I had sent it to her in my letters. I still have that picture framed by my mom with me.

If it wasn't for my school, I would have never made it this far, along with my prayers and blessing of Mother Mary. My boarding days were filled with fun and games and dancing solo with guys during feast days. I would also like to add that the studious students, which included me too, had to tutor the boarders who were weak in studies. We used to get to watch English movies every weekend. Namely all the movies of James Bond, Bruce Lee and Jackie Chang along with classical one like, the Chariots of fire, Benhur, Passion of Christ, Gandhi, Sound of music, Peles Escape to Victory and many more. These were great moments we cherished of our Boarding days.

I thank God every day for giving me the opportunities to study in such an esteemed Institution which was run by Salesians of Don Bosco, started by Italian Father Maschio in Mumbai more than a hundred years ago. The Shrine of St Don Bosco Matunga is a beautiful place of worship made from within from Italian marbles imported from Italy and the crypt below the Shrine is also beautiful designed with Italian marbles along with relics of Saints. We used to hear mass there every day during our Boarding days which was such a peaceful experience for me. Though one day me and another boarder Ross decided to skip mass and go straight to the refectory for breakfast. Which led to both of us being kicked out of the boarding just few months before our crucial final exams of 10th grade. It taught me one precious lesson of not missing mass, especially on Sundays come what may.

My school till today has the best sporting complex in the whole of Mumbai. You have to see it to believe it. It includes a full seize Astro turf hockey ground, two full seize turf football ground, one cricket ground, two synthetic surface tennis Court, one full seize football ground and innumerable basketball courts. The Prestigious annual Basketball tournament named Savio Cup is held every year in my school. It has its own Sport academy called Bosco Academy where Moscow Olympics, gold medal winning team Player Sir Somaiya is the CEO along with another international player Mr. Edgar Mascarenhas being the Director of sports of the International school of Don Bosco, Matunga, Mumbai. I was fortunate to play an exhibition match with ex Indian players against the players of St Don Bosco team the day the academy was inaugurated.

I remember watching the prestigious Agha Kan hockey tournament finals at Mahindra Hockey stadium where our school defeated St Stanislous School Bandra, Mumbai our arch rivals 3-2, in which Edgar was the star player along with Simon Pascal and other great players. I was in the seventh grade and was filled with pride when our school lifted the Prestigious Agha Kan Interschool hockey trophy. It's a dream come true for anyone pursuing a sporting career to be in this school.

It's a real proud feeling to be from such historic school who had alumni as Bollywood stars Sashi Kapoor, Akshay Kumar (we used to call him Rajiv Bhatia) who was from my brother's batch along with Ravi Shastri 1983 Cricket world cup winner. India's first World Cup in one day Cricket in Lords, England. Later Jatin Paranjpe who played for Mumbai in Ranji's trophy and represented India too was from my school. I was fortunate to meet him on a few occasions on our school grounds.

We also have Shreyas Iyer as the latest sensation of the Indian cricket team along with junior Edgar Mascarenhas, who too represented India in hockey as a goalkeeper as our school's alumni. I had the fortune of playing Badminton with Shreyas Iyer, who is a fierce competitor even in the racquet sports of badminton, along with Bollywood actress Sayami Khere. Both of whom are excellent badminton players, who come to join us while we play badminton at MCA club in BKC Mumbai.

We also have the present Cabinet Minister Piyush Goyal of the Indian Government headed by Prime Minister Honorable Mr. Naresh Modi as the alumni of this prestigious school who heaped praises for our school on his visits to a function in school few years back.

I made a few close friends namely Vitreous, Jonathan, Boris, Dominic, Ashley, Vinod, Jai Kishen, Malcolm, Sanjay and many more, who were close to me even today and most of us still make it a point to meet during our reunion every year.

The boarding life instilled discipline, team work and being independent making us boy's survivors in all situations in life that we were to face ahead of us.

Chapter 4

LIFE IN XAVIER'S COLLEGE, MUMBAI

When I reflect on the challenges of getting admission, into a prestigious college like Xavier's, I am filled with immense pride of doing it by myself. My entry into this esteemed institution, run by the Jesuit Fathers and headed by the then Rector, Fr. Misquitta SJ, it felt like a true blessing from God and my school, St. Don Bosco, Matunga in Mumbai. Thanks to my school's support, I was allowed to take the aptitude test to secure admission to St. Xavier's College, Mumbai.

The transition from an all-boys school to a co-ed college with a majority of students coming from affluent backgrounds was quite a culture shock for me. I found myself surrounded by kids of industrialists, famous lawyers, Bollywood actors, and other well-known personalities. Among them were Bosky, daughter of Rakhee Gulzar, Rahul Khanna, son of Vinod Khanna. And the many others who passed through this college. I also came across Glen my classmate and one of the hockey and football players in our college team and the son of the founder of Glenmark Pharmaceuticals' company. Glen was a down-to-earth and friendly guy, and I was fortunate to buy a few shares in his company, which has since performed well in the markets, thanks to his achievements of making his company so successful and mostly for being humble and a good human being always. I have attended few of his annual parties he keeps for his friends and met him on few occasions in Cavalla on Friday nights at Goa. He is still the same humble person I met in a college.

Out of all these notable individuals, the one who left the deepest impact on me was Sachin Tendulkar's wife, Anjali Mehta. Anjali was not only my classmate but also one of the best human beings and kindest souls, I had ever met in my life. We both took up Russian language in Xavier's whose classes used to held at Kemps Corner in the House of Soviet Culture, which was very close to her place on Bhulabhai Desai Road. Her spacious bungalow, situated opposite the US Consulate, was like a mansion and the first of its kind that I had ever visited. Getting to know her and her lovely, humble family was a dream come true. We often played hangman games on the blackboard during our Russian lectures, and I always managed to get myself hanged, which amused Anjali. She invited me to her house once to see the Christmas tree her mom had set up, and I still remember the delicious chocolate cake her mom and cousin had baked. Anjali's heart of gold was evident when she gifted her home maid's gold chains on her 18th birthday which party, I had a honour of attending. I vividly remember all of us taking a ride in a white gypsy after her birthday party on Marine drive through the queen necklace road facing the sea, all her friends were having a beer and she offered me beer which I refused. That day I realized that I would never touch alcohol, as I had promised my mom. I realized that, when I could refuse a beer from the most beautiful girl in my college then I was sure no one else could ever make me drink alcohol my entire life. I visited her place once more with a close friend, Atul, after I joined Mumbai Customs. But after that have not been in touch with this good soul except when I met her at airport on one occasion while she was travelling. I was happy to find out, that she was the same person I met in Xavier's, a graceful and beautiful human being.

I was overjoyed to learn that she married the cricketing legend, Sachin Tendulkar. Especially knowing that she also had first set eyes on him, from the same viewing gallery at Sahar International Airport, Mumbai, where I had seen my mother being harassed by Customs officers. This incident had led me to decide to become a Customs officer to help my mom and others who faced similar situations. Our destinies changed through the same viewing gallery for the better in our own individual lives were we made our dreams come true and are living our happy married life for more than two decades.

On a funny note, there was a incident during my time at Xavier's when I encountered three pretty girls walking towards me in the corridor. One of them suddenly fainted, and I caught her before she hit the ground. Not realizing that my pants tore at the back while lifting her. Nevertheless, I carried her through the corridors and down the stairs to the ground floor, where her friends took her home in a taxi. I never saw her again but was glad to know she was fine.

Xavier's College was replete with iconic locations such as the Victorian library, a beautiful chapel, canteen with a wide variety of dishes, the basketball and volley ball courts where the students played. It also had a great indoor badminton court and gym. These places felt like heaven for the students and served as meeting points where many lasting friendships were forged. I spent countless hours studying in the Victorian library, with its beautiful cubicles and extensive book collection which were available for rent. The canteen foyer was a vibrant and happy place, hosting social dances, prom nights, and Xavierite night dances, where we danced the night away with good friends like Natasha, Sharon, and Anna who loved to dance.

The college hall witnessed numerous events, including the renowned Malhar Intercollegiate festival, where colleges from all over Mumbai and beyond participated in cultural and sports activities. Xavier's College offered a wide array of activities and clubs, like the Social Service League (SSL), which engaged in various social responsibility initiatives like having blood donations drive. They also arranged lovely treks to the hill stations of Mumbai like Matheran and Khandala.I remember one of these during the rainy season, where we left at midnight in the last train to karjat and slept in the night on platform a stop before matheran called Nerul I think. We woke up early morning and trekked on to the hills to Matheran. The clouds kissing us when we reached higher. The beautiful waterfalls we ran into to get wet. The lovely greenery below us when we reached on top of the mountains. The hot chai with bajyas and wadas we had at the end of our trek. The climb down from matheran to the station to take us back home in the Mumbai locals. These memories are priceless and will be with us for the rest of our lives.

The music department produced talents like Ustad Zakir Hussain and his brother, Alla Rakha. I was fortunate to meet Zakir Hussain at Mumbai Airport while working as a Customs officer. He too was a gem of a person who took the time to chat with me before his flight took off. In fact he was enjoying our chat so much that his assistant had to drag him away so that he wouldnt miss his flight.

Xavier's College boasted an impressive list of alumni, including Bollywood legends like Farooque Sheikh, Naseeruddin Shah, Shabana Azmi, Satish Shah and Vidya Balan and Journalist Rajdeep Sardesai who owns a leading News Channel at present . Models like Rhea Pillai, Cyrus Bharucha, Shenaz Tresurywalla and Sports personalities like Sir Somaiya, who represented the Gold medal winning Indian hockey team in the 1980 Moscow Olympics. Sunil Gavaskar, a legendary cricketer and a Xavierite, played for the college team and won accolades in intercollegiate cricket tournaments and was also the winner of the first Prudential World Cup in Lords in 1983 along with having an illustrious career in Cricket.

I am immensely grateful to every teacher at Xavier's who imparted knowledge to me, but I must give a special thanks to a fellow student named Tushar Kamat. He helped me grasp abstract subjects like math's and statistics, when I had to change my original choice of subjects from physics, chemistry, and geology to Maths, Statistic and economics to accommodate my hockey practices which clashed with my science practicals My routine for every day of my college life till the thirteenth grade, was to wake up at 7 am, take the Mumbai local to Victoria terminus in South end of Mumbai, walk to my college from there. Then after college take BEST Bus nos 84 and go to Kemps Corner for Russian lecture. From there leave for hockey practice to Khandhivali in the north of Mumbai at Mahindras ground. Then take Mumbai local again to reach Dadar station zin center of Mumbai. I then changed another train to go to kurla station, where my residence was tired and exhausted. My journey took me from central to south Mumbai then to North Mumbai and back to central Mumbai till I reached my place in Kurla.I did this schedule for more than two years till I joined Mumbai Customs hockey team who fortunately practiced hockey in my school. Where we trained hard under the guidance and coaching of Mukul Sir who was instrumental in getting me.my dream job in Mumbai Customs. My hard work and dedication paid off when I secured a place in my dream team, Mumbai Customs hockey team, after completing the 13th grade. From that point on, there was no looking back to my dream job as a Customs officer at Mumbai Customs fulfilling, my second promise I had made to my loving mom.

Chapter 5

LIVING MY DREAMS

Throughout my career in the Customs Department, I remained dedicated to my passion for sports and continued playing hockey and later took up badminton. Being in the sports quota, I had the opportunity to participate in various tournaments, and some of our most memorable wins were at the All-India Central Revenue Sports Meet, these were like our Olympics, to us where we played against all the different Departments under CBIC (Central Board of Indirect Taxes). We clinched gold medals three years in a row. These victories were a tribute to my hockey coach and mentor, Mukul Sir, whose coaching, and never-give-up attitude inspired us all.

Thanks to my Customs job under sports quota, I even managed to complete my Law degree (LLB) from the prestigious Government Law college in Mumbai. It was an awesome experience where I encountered students whose parents were judges and famous lawyers. I even saw Bollywood actress Kareena Kapoor try her hand in law studies in this college. Though she couldn't complete it later, due to her busy schedule in Bollywood, which she admitted to me when I met her at the Mumbai Airport, whilst I was posted there. I was so fond of law studies, that I topped the Law of Torts subject in my whole college, this despite working and playing my sports of hockey professionally.

I even completed my Masters in Law and my MBA in marketing from the SIBM school at Mumbai. If it was not for my job in Customs, I would not be able to complete the above degrees for which I am forever grateful to Mumbai Customs Department who gave me the permission to complete my studies, which helped me in my professional life at Customs while attending courts and other administrative matters in office.

During my post-divorce torrid experience, I decided to have a change of place from Mumbai to Delhi airport just to forget the pain and trauma I was going through. I along with my friend Atul applied for deputation to Delhi airport. I was selected to go to Delhi airport where a new chapter of my life was going to unfold. During my deputation to Delhi Airport, I faced several challenges, including finding suitable accommodation and coping with the harsh and polluted climate. Despite these initial difficulties, I found solace in joining Shanti Club, in Vasant Kunj in South Delhi, where I met a girl who would later become the love of my life. Despite her initial hesitancy, our friendship blossomed into a beautiful love story that has now spanned more than 22 years.

Amidst the joys of my personal life, a storm brewed in my professional life. Due to my helpful nature, I lent my mobile phone to a colleague, who used it to make a call to a passenger involved in a smuggling case without my knowledge. This innocent gesture resulted in my name being dragged into a controversy and led to my suspension for twenty-two months. During this period, I used the opportunity to pursue a course in Master's in Law, specializing in Criminal Law and Consumer Law, from Mumbai University. This proved to be a blessing in disguise, as I thoroughly enjoyed the subjects and found the legal knowledge to be of immense help while fighting my court cases.

Not only was I suspended due to the mobile phone interaction of just sixteen seconds, but also separate proceedings were initiated against me, including a Vigilance case, Show Cause Notice, and two court cases. It took me over 17 years to clear my name and prove my innocence in all these proceedings in which, thanks to my legal studies, I was able to defend myself successfully. Eventually, I received my long-overdue promotion to Assistant Commissioner of Customs in 2017, along with the arrears of pay amounting to around ten lakhs' rupees.

With the financial windfall, I fulfilled one of my dreams by taking my family on a memorable Europe tour. We visited Disneyland in Paris, enjoyed the romantic ambiance of the Eiffel Tower, explored Barcelona, and marveled at the beauty of Switzerland's Mount Titlis. These cherished memories will remain etched in our minds forever, and I am grateful that we had the opportunity to create such wonderful memories, before the onset of the COVID pandemic. Our trips to Paris were mostly filled with awe and delight, looking at the Eiffel Tower and finding the place so romantic as shown in movies. But we had few hiccups when my younger son and me decided to go by metro at Paris while returning to our hotel. We almost got robbed in the metro train by a group of thieves . They got scared when I requested to take a selfie with them and they ran out of the metro train at the next station to my relief. Later I came to know that the Paris police caught them and took them in custody. But on the whole the Europe trip especially the kids visiting the Disneyland and watching the final show of the fireworks and light show there, was a memorable experience for them. The visit to the Barcelona football team stadium was also awesome for my kid. Though me being a Real Madrid fan would have preferred going to Bernabue stadium in Madrid. But we could not make it due to the tight travel schedule to Switzerland which was awesome too especially playing in the snow at Mount Titlis.

During the pandemic thanks to my Central Government job, I was able to keep it when the rest of the world were going through job cuts especially the hotel Industry and other Industries. In fact, during the Pandemic I had a great time with my family where we used to play different games along with wife and kids, like football, hockey, badminton, and swimming in our apartment club house. Due to which we could bond well and enjoy ourselves along with keeping ourselves healthy and have positive outlook to life. Maybe that's was the reason the pandemic didn't hit us badly the way it did to so many in the world around us. Mostly I would like to thank God for keeping us safe and healthy during all the three waves of covid that hit India.

During the thirty one years that I spent in Mumbai Customs I was part of the team, which made good seizures of smuggling cases one of such instance was when I was in Rummaging and Intelligence wing, which deals with preventing of smuggling activities via sea route of the Mumbai Coastline. We had information that two hundred and fifty gold bars would be smuggled in a ship coming from the gulf sector. We boarded the ship and searched the whole ship and managed to find the two hundred gold bars in the engine room of the ship . But the remaining fifty gold bars, as per specific information received was not yet detected. We kept searching the whole day for it. After which we started to interrogate the Chief Engineer who, as per the information was involved in the smuggling. His interrogation by our team lead to the discovery of the remainder of the fifty gold biscuits. Our seizure was complete and successful thanks to our teamwork and Seniors who guided us well in performing our duties as Customs officers posted in the Intelligence wing.

In another Incident when I was posted in the Air Cargo complex (ACC). where I was posted in Central Intelligence Units of ACC, we a team of officers were sitting on a cartoon of boxes in the export shed of ACC during our lunch break. One of the officers hand just went through a cartoon box and when he removed his hand, he had a packet of mandrax tablets in his hands. The cartoon which we were sitting on was filled with mandrax tablets whose exports were banned under the NDPS Act (Narcotic Drugs and Psychotropic Substances Act, 1985). We had a seizure of drugs in our grasp for which we didn't get any specific information beforehand. But it involved great deal of work as a team to find the smugglers of the said drug. As the exporter whose name was on the shipping bills of export was not aware that drugs were being clandestinely exported instead of the declared exports. We eventually solved the case and found the actual smugglers of the drugs.

When I was posted later, once again in ACC after a few years, while I was handling courier services import and export sections as an Appraising Officer, we detected Eighteen kgs of gold concealed in transformers in plate form. We handed the case over to Directorate of Revenue Intelligence (DRI) who later concluded that this gold was smuggled in transformers, thirty-eight times previously too. We were the ones who, detected it the last time it was illegally imported and brought the gold smuggling to an end at courier cell in ACC.

During my last posting as Head of the Air Intelligence Unit of Goa Customs in Dabolim Airport, I was fortunate to have a good team of officers working under me who detected 2 gold smuggling cases of 2 kg of gold each, in gold paste form. The first case was of one concealed by a passenger on his tummy stuck with tape and in the second case it was concealed in the toilet of an Air India aircraft. This gold was detected by the AIU team, on search of the Air craft on its arrivals from gulf country.

In another instance the same officers who had been working the whole day on a foreign currency case for more than twelve hours at a stretch, at around 2 am during the night shift they, detected one kg cocaine worth five crores concealed by Kenyan passenger in his hand baggage. The same officers, detected another drug case of one kg worth three crores' rupees, within a week again with a lady traveling from South African country once again. I was honored and privileged to be working with these officers during my tenure at Goa International Airport at Dabolim, where we facilitated genuine passengers at the airport but caught those who were trying to smuggle goods in and out of India illegally.

As I reflect on my life's journey, I am thankful for the support and love of my family and the strength to overcome the challenges that came my way. My dream of a loving family and fulfilling career has become a reality, and I am excited to see what new adventures and opportunities life has in store for me, where I plan to open my own law firm in Mumbai so that I can put my Law degrees to good use by helping those who are fighting for justice.

Chapter 6

MY LOVE LIFE - THE THORNS WITH THE ROSES OF LIFE

Love is best defined in the Bible in Corinthians chapter 12 and 13.

Love is patient and kind; love does not envy or boast; it is not arrogant or rude. It does not insist on its own way; it is not irritable or resentful; it does not rejoice at wrongdoing, but rejoices with the truth. It doesn't keep count of wrongs of loved ones.

I always wanted to find a love like that my whole life, unaware that you encounter a few wrong people before you find the right one. The same thing happened to me. Being from a boys' school, I was so shy around girls when I joined St. Xavier's College, Mumbai. Hockey was my first love. During my whole college life, even though, there were such beautiful girls in Xavier's, I never got distracted or left my love for Hockey and studied hard to achieve my dreams. In addition to my love to jive at all the shows in college, which remains one of my passions till date, thanks to my Anglo and Goan bloodline. My Dad was an Anglo Indian and mom a Goan.

I had decided that I would get friendly with a girl only when I got a job. In college, I had crushes on a few girls whom I never disclosed that I liked them, but later in life, when I connected with them, they happened to know about my crushes towards them.

The first time I was friendly with a girl was at twenty-one, after becoming a Customs officer. It was more out of lust than love for her. I even remember the day I lost my virginity, it was my mother's birthday, 18.4.1992, at Fonseca's shack at Goria beach. Your first time should be special, but this never felt like that. It felt like a mystery. I don't regret it though as it was a part of learning experience for me. I did it as I was upset with my mom for leaving me and staying in Dubai, even though I had a great job, due to which I could have taken good care of her. I even helped her to get her own place in Mumbai. But she preferred staying in Dubai as she wanted to take care of my half-sister Zeenat and my half-brother Adin who were very small. They were born much later as my mom had to protect herself from advances of the Arabs living in Dubai, after my dad's death being very young. She remarried a Keralite Indian, whom sadly I always hated as I never wanted anyone to replace my dad. I always called him uncle as my father was the only one I wanted to call Dad . That was also the reason that I hated my uncle as I felt he took my mom away from me for the rest of my life. My half sisters and brothers were close to me though and loved me very much.

I lived most of my life alone. Lonely lamb, I used to call myself sometimes; Queen's famous song "Living on my Own" applied to me fully. I always heard it during my bachelor days and loved to dance on it. During all the shows that I attended at our different clubs and Gymkhanas in Mumbai and Bengaluru.

My first run in a relationship did not last long as my mom didn't like her, so I broke it off within seven months. That was the last time I let my mom make my decisions, on my love matters.

Then one day, one of my good friends Elizabeth, from Xavier's while being dropped somewhere by me, decided to visit another of our friend, Candice, from Xavier's living on Mahakali road Andheri.

I never knew this detour would change my life. It was going to be my first entry into the deep anguish and pain for being in love. It was a dream in the beginning, but it turned into a nightmare in the end.

I visited her for the first time after leaving college with Elizabeth. She was my first true love. I had fallen head over heels from the first time I saw her at her place.

I would go to see her at night, climbing over the scaffolding that was laid in her building while it was getting renovated. We used to meet in her bedroom without her parents knowing about it.

She had just been out of a relationship with a guy who seemed to be the controlling type, and so much so that, one day, he sent some goons to scare me. But my colleagues and good friends Alok and Tolia came to my rescue before anything untoward happened to me.

That day, I requested her to choose between me or the ex-boyfriend. Luckily, she chose me, and our love took off from there.

There was not a day that I didn't see her and spend each and every second of my life with her. We went to beaches in Mumbai for long walks, under the moon light and sunsets, Christmas dances, Valentine dances. Life was a bed of roses. It was a dream come true. We were friendly for a year and a half, which flew by like I was in heaven. During which time, I stopped talking to all my friends, whether boys or girls, as she didn't like most of my friends. I even cut myself off from my family, mostly from my mom, as she said something bad about my love.

I was so deep in love that I didn't realize I had become a doormat, which was fatal in the end to the relationship. This is one thing you should never do in a relationship, whether a girl or boy. I learned the hard way that you should always love someone who loves you more than you love them.

I was such a fool that my marriage to her was based on the condition that I purchase a flat for her, which I did by taking a loan and putting the flat on her name without giving it a second thought, even before getting married. Only after I got her the flat was my wedding day fixed on 15.2.96, at Sacred Heart Church, Mahakali, and Reception at Crystal Springs, Bandra. It was an awesome wedding. I wanted Joshua Kadison's "Beautiful in My Eyes" to be the song for the first wedding dance, but my father-in-law wanted another song I had never heard of earlier. I always had to give in, not only to her, but also my in-laws' wishes too.

Then came the honeymoon in Goa, staying at a hotel close to Baga beach. Everything was going like a dream, but after 15 days, my in-laws landed in Goa, and my life came tumbling down. I had an argument with my sister-in-law Janice after which she took my wife and her sister away. I never spent another day or night with her after that. My fifteen days of marriage was over. My life came to a standstill. I waited alone in the hotel for a week, till our booking was over. After that, I left for Mumbai to our matrimonial home all alone. The only night we spent here after marriage was on our wedding night.

The worst was yet to come. When I went to work, they took possession of our matrimonial home, and I was left outside our matrimonial home. Thanks to my late Uncle Joseph and cousin Julius and my grandmother Mariaan Nana, I managed to get possession of the flat after police intervention. But then I got emotional and handed over both the possession and documents of the flat to a Priest Fr. Viren, who I thought would bring us together, if I gave her the flat again. But on the contrary, this same Priest helped my wife in annulling my marriage at the

Archbishop's house in Mumbai when, as per Canon Law, a marriage that is consummated cannot be declared null and void, which came as a shock to me. But I took it as God's will and took everything in my stride. I always believed that If you love someone set them free. If they come to you it's meant to be if not it wasn't meant to be. Sadly, I never felt neither me or my ex-wife did any wrong. Whatever she did was for her parents wellbeing and financial independence.That's was the reason I never had any ill feelings towards her and wished her well always.

Inspite of them along with their conniving Lawyer went to the extent of going to my Commissioner and filed a false complaint against me, that I had gone and abused my wife's sister who worked as an Air hostess, in Jet Airways at that time, which was not true. But my Commissioners mind got poisoned by their lies and he suspended me without listening to my pleas of innocence. He even coerced me to write on a blank piece of paper thrice that I had done as they alleged in their complain, to which I refused all the three times and mentioned that I didn't do anything as they had falsely alleged. He then in anger took the same piece of paper and passed an order that I may be suspended. If he had only applied his mind to realize that Air hostesses don't sit in offices, so it was not possible for me to go to her office and abuse her especially when Customs, work only in international airport when she was flying just domestic sectors. Later on, when our vigilance dept conducted inquiry, they found that I was innocent after questioning the witnesses who worked in the Jet airlines office and passed an order that my suspension was wholly unjustified. I got all my dues of.salary of my nine months of period of suspension along with the period I was suspended, being treated as on duty. But the social stigma I faced due to the false complain could never be undone. During all these times I only prayed to God to undo the injustice done to me for falling in love.

It was a real relief and divine justice especially when I even contemplated to commit suicide, when I was suspended for doing no wrong and faced social stigma of being suspended from my dream job. I realized my ex and her lawyers were harassing me so that I would agree to their false divorce grounds. I got my act together and decided to study Law from Government Law College to fight them tooth and nail. I always believed that when someone closes the door instead of banging on the door, look for the window which God will open for you. I believed in doing constructive and positive things rather than do destructive and negative things in life, like drinking and going into depression.

If it wasn't for my family and friends, I don't know how I would have gotten over this part of my life. They not only unsurped the flat, but they also spread false rumors about me to everyone they met, especially my friends. But I just prayed to God to give me the strength and will power to fight the divorce proceeding, where they filed all the grounds which were there in The Indian Divorce Act, which they could never prove. In the end after almost 4 years, when I met Shikha in Delhi, I decided to close the chapter of my divorce and agreed to the Divorce on grounds of mutual consent which was signed and sealed by the Registrar in the Family court in Bandra, Mumbai. Bringing to close an ugly chapter in my life.

The consent terms agreement, had to be produced during the last date of hearing in the High court Mumbai. But later I came to know that their wicked lawyer connived with my lawyer and got their Divorce on their original grounds exparte, since I could not attend the last date of hearing as I was posted in Delhi and in good faith had appointed my lawyer to attend court on my behalf. This was a grave miscarriage of Justice towards me.

But till today I have the mutual consent terms of agreement on the basis of which the divorce was granted, along with the evidence to prove my innocence. That's the reason they didn't bother to implement the order till date. Now almost more than twenty-four years. I suffered deeply for almost four years after this breakup and being deceived in love. During all this journey of hurt, being cheated, and crushed in love, I never lost my faith in love and prayed to God to give me the strength to become stronger from it. One of my friends told me once that in love, you have to shed tears of blood. That's what had exactly happened to me. God heard my prayers when I went on a deputation posting to IGI Airport in Delh in 1999.

Life in Delhi was very lonely at first. I used to fly to Mumbai every day after work and return the next day for my duty. In six months, I had flown more than two hundred times (I used to go and meet my mom who had returned with my half-sister as needed their support and care), which took a toll on my health, so I decided to reduce my travel time and spend time in Delhi. I joined a club called Shanti club in Vasant Kunj in South Delhi. It was the best thing I did in my entire life. I love swimming, so I decided to join the club. There one day I met a beautiful girl with the most lovely green eyes, I had ever seen in my life. Along with it, she had the deepest dimple when she smiled. I drowned in it the first time I saw her. In my wildest dreams, I never imagined she would be my wife one day in the near future. But I always believed that God makes all things beautiful in his time, and my time had come to embrace something beautiful after four long years of pain and agony.

God works His miracles in His marvelous ways. My wife Shikha never liked swimming, but her relatives forced her to join the club to swim along with her two little cousins, Himanshi and Rahul. I used to hate Delhi but was posted there because of the initiative from my friend Atul. We met due to the divine plan of God. It was an awesome union of two good souls. Initially Shikha was not keen on getting into a relationship as her conservative family would never have allowed our union.

She told me that she could be my friend and nothing more. I told her, I have so much love to give and no one to give it to. I kept pursuing her. I spent all my free time with her, which I had lots of as I was suspended the second time again for no fault of mine. But this was a blessing in disguise as it gave me lots of time with the one, I loved. We spent hours together in her management school, which was on Qutub Minar Road. The lovely time we spent on the roadside Dhabas in the rainy season, especially having egg rolls and Maggie with hot chai, were the best times of my life. Spending evenings around Qutub Minar and other historical places in Delhi.

We even went to her friend Pooja's resort in the middle of Jim Corbett National Park, in cottages which had glass ceilings along with few couples who studied with her. We made love the whole night under the moonlight. This happened only when Shikha fell in love with me on 11th November 2000. It was like being in heaven. My happiness and joy knew no bounds. I think we were three couples dating then who had come for, the excursion there. Later in life all were romantically married to each other. It was a lucky cottage for me and all her friends there.

The mobiles had just come into the Indian market. I gifted Shikha with Siemens C35 mobile so that we could keep in touch always. We began dating and spending lots of time together. Days turned to nights, and we couldn't be separated even for a day. So much so, that she didn't want to take a rickshaw when she finished her college and had to go home. I told her to go in the auto, but she insisted we go on my bike.

On that fateful day while I was dropping her home, a stone came under a truck driving next to us and hit the front wheel of my bike. I couldn't control the bike and flew off from it, with Shikha on my back. This happened on JNU Road, and thank God the vehicle behind us didn't run us over. It was a miracle. Shikha got a few bruises on her hand, and I, once again, was unhurt one more miracle in my life for which I have God to thank, along with prayers of my mom which protected me always from all dangers that I encountered in my life.

Shikha hadn't told anyone in her family that we were dating, so she had to lie that she fell down and bruised herself while playing basketball. During our dating days, we had so many close calls with her relatives passing us while we were driving in my car. Had they known we were dating, our union would have ended right there.

We kept seeing each other for more than a year until the fateful day when I was transferred back to Mumbai from my deputation in Delhi airport after 3 years. I knew her relatives would never agree to our union. Therefore, I told her that if she really loved me, she had to come to Mumbai. I told her just to come in the clothes she was wearing and her important educational documents.

When I left Delhi, I never imagined she would take such a leap from the family she loved and cherished, to come to me. But I had faith in God that she would do the right thing so that our love could be complete together culminating in our wedding.

She came to Mumbai as she had promised. I requested one of my colleagues to escort her on the flight and arranged, for her air ticket to Mumbai. I still remember it was 4th October 2001. She landed in an Air India flight in just the outfit she was wearing and her documents.

The next day, we went to the family court in Bandra. I caught a lawyer passing by and asked him under which Act I could get married immediately. He advised me to do it under The Hindu Marriage Act as there was a notice period of 30 days in The Special Marriage Act. We got married under The Hindu Marriage Act and got our Marriage certificate on the same day.

The very next day, by the time we left for our close friend Vitreous place in Mudh Island, I had a feeling that my in-laws would come to search for us, as her relatives were in Delhi police. They came to Mumbai, the next day with a super cop, her uncle, along with her dad, who went to all my residences in Mumbai and inquired about our whereabouts. They managed to find my neighbors who were witnesses to our Hindu marriage and threatened them with dire consequences if they didn't tell them about our whereabouts.

Fortunately, her dad and uncle had no idea about our Mudh Island hideout and couldn't get any information to find us. Just to put them off, we sent an email that we had left for Dubai. They even went to my best friend Atul's place, but he advised them that their daughter was in safe hands and that they should not cause any harm either to me or Shikha.

They returned home empty-handed, sad and disappointed not to find their daughter.

We lived happily in our married life until one day I saw my wife sobbing. She was missing her family to whom she was closely knit. I told her to call them and tell them she is safe with me in Mumbai.

She called them and told them we are happily married. But her grandmother, who everyone called Bibi, had a strong influence on her entire family. She made sure that no one harmed us. She had promised me that she would get us married in front of her family and friends. We met her family who were hurting from inside but welcomed me. Her grandmother was the rock and foundation of her family. She made sure that no one harmed us. She just requested time to arrange for the wedding in Delhi, so that they could send off their daughter happily with all their family and friends to witness it.

I was told to return to my place. I left for Mumbai and waited patiently for two months, at times dreading the worst that they would get my wife married to someone else, or worse, even take her life, as done in her village to couples for dishonoring the family by marrying someone outside their religion.

Shikha, stayed back in Delhi and prepared for our wedding. Bibi kept her promise and organized a grand wedding at Taj Mahal Hotel, Chanakyapuri, Delhi, on 8th December 2001. My family couldn't make it due to unavoidable circumstances, But my friends and colleague, Vinod who acted as my brother during the marriage and helped me out immensely along with his wife and kids, and my close family friends Iona aunty, Austin Uncle, and their kids Diana, Natalie, and Kimberly were there to grace the occasion. They even decorated their cars as my wedding car.

The reception was held in a beautiful hall, and the Hindu wedding rituals were conducted on the lawns of Taj. I was wearing a cream-colored sherwani, and my beautiful bride was wearing an exquisite wedding lehenga, looking radiant with her dimples and green eyes. We both were happy that everything went smoothly during the wedding celebrations.

In the end, all went well with a few hiccups from drunk guests. They say a wedding is for a day, but marriage is for a lifetime. It's been more than twenty-two years today. Our lives just flew by with two lovely handsome sons. Our lives had its ups and downs in terms of my professional life, but we have stuck together through thick and thin. The difference in our age is ten years, but it seems to have worked in our benefit, as our maturity levels match. In the twenty-two years that we have been together, we have not fought even once. The main reason for that is that when my wife talks in anger, I never reply but stay silent, as I believe that in these circumstances, silence is golden. Also, when I am angry, I prefer not speaking, as what you say in anger, if hurtful, can never be taken back. That is the reason I prefer being silent. After the anger is gone, my wife calms down and is her loving self again. She is the lion, and I am the lamb in our romance. Thank God we have been together for so long, even though we are from different religions; she is a Hindu, and I'm a Catholic. This never comes between us, and we believe that it's better to have the best of both religions and the worst of none. We celebrate all the festivals, be it Christmas or Diwali, with the same fervor, joy, and happiness. We love each other, which we believe will last for an eternity. Our kids too are growing to be good human beings. Both our sons Aarav and Vivaan are good kids. Though at times, they do fight amongst themselves but, when it comes to supporting each other, they are always on the same team. Hope and pray they grow into good human beings and achieve their dreams like I did and give some things back to society in their own loving ways.

CHAPTER 7

MIRACLES IN MY LIFE FROM THE DAY I WAS BORN

They say that when God couldn't be everywhere, he gave us our mom. What I am today is entirely because of the first miracle in my life: my mom giving birth to me. Of course, my dad was a part of it too. They both had two daughters and wanted a son. They prayed to St. Dominic Savio, and the miracle happened. They were blessed with not one but two sons, me and my elder brother Allwin. But this is only one of the many miracles that I experienced in my life time.

The next miracle was when we got admission to St. Don Bosco boarding school. Both my brother's and my life wouldn't have been the same if we didn't pass out of this prestigious institution. It was there that I learned to play football and hockey, which later in life helped me secure a job in Mumbai Customs as an Officer under sports quota. It was something I had always dreamt of, and could achieve due to my hard work in studies and sports. In addition to my mom's prayers and blessing which always showed me the right path to success.

In my life time, there were many miracles. For example, during all my Board exams and University exams, I always selected an examination center near the Shrine of St. Don Bosco in Matunga, where I always went to say a prayer before my exams, and my exams always went well.

One day during my twelfth grade Board exams since I had got my text books late I tried to study the whole physic text book staying awake the whole night, a day before my exams by lighting an agarbatti and burning myself with it every time I fell asleep.

In the morning after a small nap, I rushed for my exams. Since I was running late I didn't find time to go the Shrine of St Don Bosco Matunga which I did before each and every exam paper. During my exams my paper went so bad. I almost slept through the whole exam paper. I still remember it was Physic part two paper. I miraculous cleared the physics paper as my physic part one exams had gone well the day before when I had gone and prayed at the Shrine to Mother Mary. It must have been the combined marks of both the papers that got me through. After this I never ever missed going to prayer before any important event in my life.

Another miracle saved my life not once but more than twenty-two times, I fell from my bike or scooter, but I neither got a scratch on my body nor was any bones in my body ever broken. The reason for my rash driving was to meet the one I loved, who stayed in the north of Mumbai while I was posted in South Mumbai in the Mumbai Docks as a Customs officer. I used to rush to meet her every day, and despite the falls, I never gave up.

I even slept while driving my car on two occasions. Once, after a 15-hour night shift at Mumbai Airport in 1996, my Fiat car went over the divider and stopped in front of a light pole. The only thing that broke was my sleep. Though the car repairs cost me a fortune I was thankful that no one else was hurt. On the second occasion, I dozed off on a nice monsoon day while driving in Bengaluru. Miraculously, neither I nor the people on the road got hurt. Once again, the only thing that broke was my sleep. But the car had some major repairs which was mostly covered by insurance. Thank God for it always.

Another miracle happened when I was hanging out of a crowded local train in Mumbai during my college days. My head hit a pole, and it could have cost me my life, but I was fortunate to escape such a disaster with thirteen stitches on my head. An angel saved me that day and took me home. I never got a chance to thank that person or never heard from him mysteriously till date. I am sure, it was an angel sent from above to protect me whom, I thank every day of my life while saying my prayers.

Another miracle was when as kids in Mumbai, my brother and I had a miraculous escape from potential kidnappers while swimming in a pond close to our place. We noticed two thugs who wanted to kidnap us and we somehow escaped from there and ran naked till we reached home. If we had been kidnapped, our lives would have been miserable., like they have depicted in the Oscar winning Bollywood movie Slumdog Millionaire which depicted slum kids who are forced to beg in the streets of Mumbai, after removing their eyes or tongue.

Another miracle was getting admission to the most coveted St Xavier's College, one of the best colleges in Mumbai. It happened due to my school's tie-up with the college, where we had to give an internal aptitude test before my Board exams which I passed with flying colours due to which I could take it easy and focus on my sports activities during my Board exams.

The biggest and best miracle of my life was meeting my wife Shikha, especially after what I had been through with my earlier marriage. Our wedding was a miracle in itself as it brought together a loving non catholic girl and a Catholic boy in marriage. Our babies being born in normal delivery both times were also miracles. They are healthy and good kids, which we appreciate every day of our lives.

I remember when my second son, Vivaan, was born and was in ICU, due to pneumonia. I used to hold his tiny fingers and sing the hymn

Living waters flow on,
Wash away my pain
Bring your healing to my heart
Help me lord once again.,

....

which I believe contributed to his recovery. He has grown up to be a beautiful, kind child with a loving heart like his parents. Even now when he falls sick I take him in my arms and sing this hymn to him to sooth and comfort him.

Throughout my life, I have observed divine protection during long drives, saving me from disastrous accidents on numerous occasions. I have experienced miracles in various situations, like surviving a Air India flight tire burst and getting exonerated after seventeen years of wrongful charges at work.

I remember clearly even today the Air India Jumbo Jet was about to take off from Mumbai Airport and all of sudden brakes were applied, just before takeoff as they was a tire burst. The Pilot miraculously managed to stop the aircraft and we were saved from a major disaster on that day. We had to return to the airport and left in another aircraft.

The pandemic brought many challenges, but my family and I miraculously escaped anything grave happening to us. We enjoyed playing games together and even took part in badminton tournaments without suffering severe illnesses during the covid pandemic.

Even when I was transferred to Bengaluru, it felt like a miracle as the cool weather was refreshing compared to Mumbai's hot and humid climate. The miracle of getting a membership at Catholic Club added more joy to my life, where I made good friends and enjoyed playing sports and dancing.

There were many more miracles that happened in my life from the day I was born until today, and I could go on and on about them. I feel blessed to have experienced so many miracles in my life time. Each one leading me to greater height s and success in my life. I always felt a bubble of protection around me throughout my life, maybe it being my dad praying to God in heaven or my mom later joining him and showering me their blessings on me.and my family. These events made my faith stronger in God throughout my life. Even though I am a sinner in many ways in my life, whether by deeds or thoughts, I always pray to God for forgiveness and to make me a good person to help others along the way being my only endeavor in life. In addition, I pray to God not to hurt any human being that comes my way and to empathize with anyone going through suffering in their lives. This book is my way of giving back to society. If it leads to even one person finding his way back from despair and struggles in his life like I did, then my book has served its purpose.

Chapter 8

MY MOTTO IN SPORTS - FIT FOR LIFE

Sports has always been an integral part of my life. As a kid, I used to play a lot of cricket. I was an all-rounder, able to open the batting, bowl, and be a good fielder. I spent my days playing cricket in the maidens of Mumbai and admired Sunil Gavaskar, often imitating his style while playing with shadows as a kid.

My grandparents, who took care of me, were often frustrated as I played in my house balcony and broke walls while playing cricket. In those days, I had the opportunity to witness Sir Balwinder Sandhu, the famous Indian Cricketer, practice in our municipality ground in Nehru Nagar, Kurla East, Mumbai. Little did I know that he would be part of the Indian Cricket team that won the first Prudential World Cup for India in 1983.

During my school days at St. Don Bosco, I picked up hockey and had to choose between hockey and cricket as their seasons clashed. I chose hockey due to the immense competition in cricket. I became good at hockey and could dribble past the entire opposing team as a defender and score goals. My idol from the Indian hockey team was Pargat Singh, who inspired me to improve my skills.

I developed the skill, of dribbling as I used to take my hockey stick and ball with me to school and during the lunch break when the long corridors of our school used to be filled with kids rushing for lunch, I used to dribble past them and try to control the ball from hitting anyone who went rushing by me, till I reached the refractory for my lunch. I did this almost every day during my lunch break which eventually helped me a great deal while dribbling on the hockey grounds in school.

I remember so vividly my first hockey triumph when I played for the under 13 Hockey team of St Don Bosco, and we won the finals against our arch rivals St Stanislaus school Bandra 1-0. Few of the players like Murli and Lionel became my good friends for life as like me they too were recruited under sports quota to the Mumbai Customs

I grew stronger and improved my game as the years went by, being coached by good Coaches like Sir Naqwi and Mukul. I was made the Captain of the Under 16 school hockey team and played a vital role in winning the Fr Donnelly Cup, a memorable moment in my life. Although we won most prestigious hockey tournaments in school, we couldn't clinch the Agha Khan trophy, where we faced tough competition from St. Theresa School, Bandra, who beats us in two consecutive finals. Fortunately, after that till date, our school are winning the same trophy innumerable times.

During the Junior Nationals hockey tournament, I represented Mumbai hockey team, which was held in Kashmir and UP, I came close to being selected for the Junior India camp, but my chances faded as our team lost in the quarters to Manipur and Haryana respectively Thanks to the overaged players from these states which unfortunately happens even now. However, some of my teammates went on to represent India like the legendary goalkeeper Mark Paterson and Edward Aranha later too represented India and Air Indian hockey team.

I would like to tell you an incident while, we were leaving by train from Mumbai to Srinagar on Jammu Tavi train which takes twenty four hours to reach Srinagar, one of our goalkeepers Jude Menezez missed the train and was waiting at Borivali station, expecting our team Manager who worked in the Railways to stop the train for him by illegally pulling the chain of the train, But our Team Manager didn't pull the chain of the train and Jude had to take a flight to Delhi to take the same train at Delhi railway station.He reached Delhi before us and was waiting for us on the Railway station. He too later represented India and presently is settled In New Zealand. He is the goalkeeping coach of the National women's team.

I joined Mahindra Tractors on a stipend of Rs. 500, in 1986 my first salary. Which I offered at the altar and handed over to my mom. It helped me sustain myself during my college days, and I enjoyed having some pocket money and being a professional hockey player playing later for the Mumbai Customs hockey team in Super league of Mumbai Hockey Association. The league was held in the Mahindra stadium next to the Wankhede Stadium of Cricket.

In college, sports continued to be an important part of my life, and we won championships in football and hockey. Winning the Intercollegiate hockey tournament in the final year of Senior college was a significant achievement for us, as we beat the fancied Khalsa College 2-0 in the finals. We had just a handful of good players like Kevin and our goal keeper Denzil who was a footballer. He was made to stand as goalie for us in hockey. We had good teamwork with all the players who made us winning the trophy possible.

After joining the Mumbai Customs hockey team, I also played in the Department most important tournament, the All India Central Revenue sports meet after I was recruited under the sports quota in Mumbai Customs, where our team performed exceptionally well.

I even had the fortune of playing against hockey legend Dhanraj Pillay, when he had just joined the Mahindra's team and as a defender, we had to mark him while playing for Mumbai Customs. He was a nightmare for every defender that played opposite him. His lightning speed used to keep most of the defenders baffled.

I remember one match against him where I was playing full back, along the other defenders. Our job was to mark him during the whole match of seventy minutes. We were doing a good job of defending our citadel till the sixty-eight minutes, where he got one opening and scored an awesome goal.

He went on to win laurels for the country representing India in four Olympics and even winning the Asian games gold medal in 1998 and Asian Cup hockey championship in 2003, along with other great achievements, like the Arjuna award and many more awards bestowed on him by the nation for his achievements in the field of hockey. He always remained humble and a wonderful person throughout his life to his fellow players and fans around the world. I even played against his elder brother Ramesh Pillay who too represented India and played for RCF, Mumbai in the super league hockey tournament in Mumbai. He too was an awesome hockey player and a great personality and a good ambassador to the sports of hockey. While I played for Mumbai Customs, we also had few Olympians in our Mumbai Customs hockey team like Sir Iqbaljit Grewal and Rahul Singh and earlier we had one of the best goalkeepers of the Indian hockey team Mir Niranjan Negi who was part of the silver medal winning team in the Asian games of 1982 held in Delhi. I had an awesome time playing with and against some great hockey players during my professional career of playing hockey for Mumbai Customs hockey team like

Ivan Dacosta, Rory Fernandes, Edgar Mascarenhas and Simon Pascal all ex Boscoites and my role models while I was studying in Don Boscos.

In my early thirties, I picked up badminton, fell in love with the game, thanks to my close friend Asawari introducing me to this beautiful game. I won the first corporate games in Men's double with my colleague Tolia at Goregaon Sports complex, Mumbai. Although I never had any formal coaching in badminton, my hockey background helped me learn the game by watching and emulating my favorite players like Lee Chong Wei and Tai Tsu.I also won a Gold Medal in the men's singles 50 plus event in the Mumbai Games held at Andheri Sports Complex in 2020. In Goa too I won Gold in the Men's Double and Mixed Doubles events in the Goa state championship, held at Campal and Manohar Parrikar Stadiums respectively in 2022.

Unfortunately, my body suffered from back injuries and knee trouble due to playing badminton, but I continued with other forms of physical activity such as swimming, working out in the gym, and practicing yoga. I also never gave up on badminton and still play with the same fervor and enthusiasm. It is such an addictive game and brings so much fun and joy especially while making many good friends along the way.

I believe that everyone should engage in sports or physical activity, no matter how busy life gets. It has kept me healthy and happy throughout my life. I'm thankful for my job in Customs and GST under sports quota, which allowed me to play the games I love.

My wife who plays badminton and, represented India in the World Masters at Spain in 2020. I continue to play badminton, and I hope my kids will follow the sports-for-life culture and stay fit like us. Being healthy is a precious gift, as emphasized during the pandemic, where both rich and poor faced untimely death.

Life is short we should make the most of it by always keeping our bodies healthy. They say body is the temple of the soul. I hope we all take good care of our health, which will always be greater than all the wealth we try to accumulate during our lifetimes. which sadly we must leave behind when our time is up on this earth.

Chapter 9

MY PASSION FOR DANCE

Dancing was ingrained in my Anglo and Goan blood. My mom, dad, and my dad's sister, Violet aunty, along with her husband, Joseph's uncle, used to go to Byculla Mechanics for dance. Joseph's uncle was a great dancer and used to win dance contests at Byculla Mechanics, earning the Air India Maharaj statue as a trophy. My aunty Violet was the one who first introduced us to the joy of dancing. She used to live with us and made us dance for an hour every day, instilling discipline in us, much like our boarding school days.

Her advice was to dance as if no one was watching, and as innocent kids, we danced in our own unique ways, thoroughly enjoying it. Over time, this passion for dancing turned into something very close to my heart and soul.

When I was transferred to Bengaluru as an Assistant Commissioner of GST/Customs, being a Catholic, I had the opportunity to dance on various occasions such as Christmas, New Year, and Easter dances in our parish or church shows annually. I also became a service member of Catholic Club Bengaluru and continued my passion for dancing. The Christmas celebrations at the club were especially grand, and there were events every day, in the month December, including the Cake and Wine dance, which was a great experience culminating with the grand New Year dance to bring in the New Year.

Dancing became a way of life, not just for me but also for my brother Allwin, who was an excellent dancer. I remember him imitating Michael Jackson's moves in a red Michael Jackson Jacket, a gift from my mom. Breakdance was a big hit among the boarders in Don Bosco, and on feast days, we would have dance parties where we boys danced solo with joy. These parties were so much fun, and we danced for hours without getting tired. He is a great Salsa dancer too which he practiced for many years in the various club of Vancouver. He even took me to a dance workshop at a club , when I visited him in 2019. we had a blast there dancing to the music of salsa.

In Xavier's College, dancing with girls was a new experience. Thanks to my sisters Josephine and Leena, I knew a few steps of Jive, and I eventually gathered the courage to ask girls to dance with me. Though we knew just three steps of Jive, we danced the whole night during college dance shows like Social, Prom, and Xavierite nights that lasted till 5 am. Afterward, we would go to the Parsi Dairy Farm near Marine Lines station for hot milk and sweets to cherish those unforgettable college days.

I made some close friends in college like Natasha, Sharon, and Anna, who shared the same passion for jiving to rock and roll numbers. We had a rocking time jiving for the five years at Xavier's College, forming bonds that would last a lifetime.

Even after college, my passion for dancing continued, and I made sure to attend as many dances as possible. I became a life member of Wellington Catholic Club in Mumbai and also frequented Bandra Gymkhana for dances every Wednesday and Friday. The crowd in Bandra was fantastic, and I made more friends who shared the same love for dancing like Suzie, Jack, Vanessa, Elden and many more good friends along the way. My Jive partner Suzie and her daughter who loved to jive too was another person I would like to write about as she was the one, who always danced with me with a smile even if she was tired working the whole day at office.

I would also like to mention few musicians who made our dancing a pleasure like Michael and Sunita along with the others singers and bands in Mumbai. Similarly in Catholic club in Bengaluru Mike and a Pilot whose name I never remember played some awesome music, which used to make our feet crave to dance. The favourite bands of Goa like A26 and many others, who used to play their music on most of the shows of Catholic club in Bengaluru. Where the shows were a real joy to be part of dancing from noon to midnight.

Dancing became an essential part of my life, and I found joy in it even as I turned fifty. It was a passion that never faded, regardless of how tired or injured I was. My feet would start tapping whenever I heard my favorite numbers, and I would be ready to dance, even in the middle of the night.

My wife, though not a jive enthusiast, always allowed me to dance with other women at the club, understanding that dancing was my true passion. Also, me being a Lamb, the women I jived with always felt safe. Jiving and taking selfies were my only objective and passions.

My wife and I had won a jive contest on New year dance in Renaissance Hotel, Powai. Our gift was unlimited Fosters Beers, to be had during the whole dance. She was so sporting about dancing as she had a partial tear of ACL on the knee, due to a scooter fall. Yet she danced the whole night with me. Even if it meant undergoing a surgery the next day for fully torn ACL due to the dancing.

During my postings in Goa, I found that dances were not just limited to weekends but were held throughout the week. Different pubs like Cantare, Cohiba Cavalla, hosted dance nights on

Mondays Wednesday and Fridays respectively, I also discovered new places to jive and have a great time in Goa. Since I was living on my own during my posting in Goa Customs, as my family preferred staying in the cool Bengaluru City.

Now that my knee is not in good shape due to wear and tear of sports especially badminton I am planning to learn the ballroom dances along with Salsa, Kuzumba and Bachata provided my wife too take classes along with me. I hope and pray it works out someday.

Dancing has been a constant source of joy and a way to keep my sanity intact through life's ups and downs. Dancing, especially the jive has been one of my greatest destressers and joy of life.

Chapter 10

EMBRACING LIFE'S OBSTACLES AND TURNING THEM INTO STEPPING STONES OF SUCCESS

In writing about my life, I want to focus on the important events, especially the moments of despair and sadness, and how I transformed obstacles into stepping stones of success. My motivation for sharing my experiences is to serve as an example for others who may encounter similar challenges in their lives. I hope that my story will inspire people to stay positive, be constructive, and avoid becoming bitter, anti-social, or negative, as it can be detrimental to both individuals and society at large.

My mother taught me the invaluable lesson of never giving up and fighting through life's hardships. Her strength and determination were evident when she faced the loss of my father at an early stage in her life. From childhood, I imbibed her fighting spirit and never-say-die attitude, which guided me through various challenges in my life. I even tell my kids never to give up, even if they don't get good marks in their exams. What's important is that they do their best and leave the rest in God hands. I even jokingly tell them, their sports quota kids and to do well in sports so that doors open up to them professionally like it did for me. I hope they have a balanced life in studies and sports like I did . My good wishes and blessing are on them always.

When I joined St. Xavier's College, many advised me to join Khalsa College, known for its sports orientation. However, I chose Xavier's and remained unaffected by the peer pressure to indulge in smoking, drinking, or drugs. My strong will power and the promise I made to my mother kept me on the right path, and I never succumbed to any vices. Even to this day, I cannot stand the smell of smoke, and I am grateful for the self-discipline instilled in me.

I have started my life from scratch. I am a self-made man, when I wanted even a cycle, I purchased it with my own money from the stipend I got playing hockey for Mahindra tractors. Even my first car I purchased from my salary even though it was a second-hand car. My first home was purchased by the loan, I took from the bank, which eventually I repaid. I have lived my life on my own terms. Never ever being afraid of thinking what the world would think of me. As I realized very early in life, at the tender age of four when my dad passed away, that in your deepest despair this cold world never comes to your aid. But they are the first ones to pull you down when you are doing well in life. Therefore, all my life I did things my own way, so far as my conscience was clear. I never feared anyone from this world except God, whether be it in my personal or professional life. Even if at times I may have had to pay a price for it. I remember my mom saying to me you lay your bed and lie on it. Which is similar to the saying, "You reap what you sow."

My passion for sports never waned, and I excelled in hockey, playing at the National level for Mumbai and representing the Mumbai Customs Hockey team for over two decades. Later, I ventured into badminton, participating in numerous National events across India and forming lifelong friendships along the way.

A vital aspect of my life has been the power of prayer and the wisdom to know what I can and cannot control. The Serenity Prayer has been a guiding light during difficult times, and I have found strength in surrendering problems to a higher power while proactively seeking solutions. I also believed in the Three P s of life which are Prayers, Patience, and Perseverance. It helped me to find success during my difficult times and overcome whatever was thrown at me by this world at large.

The most trying phase of my life was the bitter divorce, which left me broken and devastated. However, I chose not to hold any grudges and wished the best for my ex-wife. With time, I found healing and love again in my life with my wife Shikha, who brought joy and two wonderful children, Aarav, and Vivaan, into my life. My sons are the embodiment of love and have been a source of immense happiness.

While I had plans of migrating to Canada to be with my brother, which is another dream. I may venture out to fulfill someday I realized the importance of spending time with my children while they were young. Family was always my priority even before my dream job, and I cherished every moment with them, playing sports and being there for their milestones. Though my life has seen its share of pain and suffering, I have learned to smile through adversity and have faith in a higher power. Having the faith that God will make all things beautiful in life, in his time.

Throughout my journey, I have turned obstacles into stepping stones by pursuing education during challenging times. I completed my LLB, LLM, and MBA from Mumbai University, which not only broadened my knowledge but also enriched my network of friends. I have learned the importance of knowledge and how it can empower an individual in different situations.

My life has been a testament to the power of faith, patience, and positivity. I believe that God only burdens us with what we can bear, and I have faced each trial with resilience. Maintaining a positive outlook has been essential, and I hope that my book will inspire readers to count their blessings and approach life with gratitude and happiness.

I always strongly believe that we should look at the white page of life and not at the black dot in the middle, which life offers along the way. But sadly, many in this world of ours, just look at the black dot of life on a white page of life, and prefer to be unhappy and disgruntled with life always.

Through this book, I aspire to share the lessons I have learned and provide encouragement to those facing challenges. May it serve as a beacon of hope and inspire others to embrace life with strength, courage, and a never-give-up attitude.

END OF BOOK.

DOWN THE MEMORY LANE

Savio Lamb of Bombay Customs prevents RCF's Ramesh Pillay, almost sprawled on the ground, from having a crack at the goal. — Express photo

Don Bosco Matunga football under 15 Winners of MSSA Inter-School Tournament

Gold medal for Mumbai Customs In 92 at All India Customs Revenue Sport meet ,Delhi

Air India's Edward Aranha slices his way through Bombay Custom defenders Rory Fernandes (extreme left) and Savio Lamb (3) while Air India's Stephen Pereira (right) waits in anticipation of a pass *(Match report on page 11)*

Bombay Customs

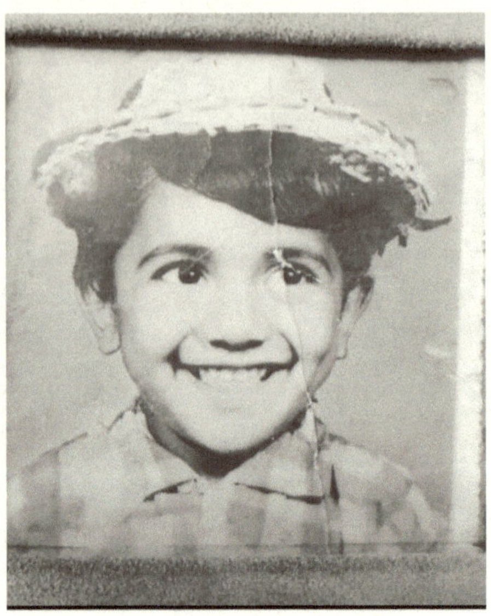

Childhood

Me with my sons Aarav and Vivaan

My wife Shikha and our two precious kids

Small Joys of Life

Me with Anjali Tendulkar(My ex-classmate in Xavier)

Vancouver Trip

Don Bosco Hockey Turf

Agha Kan Inter-school Hockey Tournament Runner-up Trophy

Me in Uniform

My Family

My Parent's Weding

The St Xavier's hockey team after their triumph in the Inter-College league

SAI schools

St Xavier Hockey Team

Don Bosco, Matunga have youngsters who on their day, can beat anyone. They proved it last month when they won the football titles in the Under-13, Under-15, and Under-17 tournaments in Bombay. The three teams above make a happy picture

Tournament Bombay

www.ingramcontent.com/pod-product-compliance
Lightning Source LLC
LaVergne TN
LVHW041132150826
845673LV00007B/2282

* 9 7 9 8 8 9 0 6 7 9 4 0 6 *